Simon and Garfunkel
Bridge Over Troubled Water

Piano/Vocal

Baby Driver, 30

Bridge Over Troubled Water, 2

Bye Bye, Love, 44

Cecilia, 10

El Condor Pasa, 7

Keep The Customer Satisfied, 14

So Long, Frank Lloyd Wright, 17

Song For The Asking, 46

The Boxer, 22

The Only Living Boy In New York, 33

Why Don't You Write Me?, 39

Exclusive distributors:

Hal Leonard
7777 West Bluemound Road, Milwaukee, WI 53213
Email: info@halleonard.com

Hal Leonard Europe Limited
42 Wigmore Street Maryleborne, London, WIU 2 RN
Email: info@halleonardeurope.com

Hal Leonard Australia Pty. Ltd.
4 Lentara Court Cheltenham, Victoria, 9132 Australia
Email: info@halleonard.com.au

Printed in EU.

www.halleonard.com

Bridge Over Troubled Water

Words and Music by
PAUL SIMON

Moderate, not too fast, like a spiritual

Rubato

When you're wea - ry,— feel - in_____ small,
down and out,— When you're on the street,

When tears are in your eyes,— I'll dry them_ all;
When eve - ning falls so hard_ I will com - fort_ you.

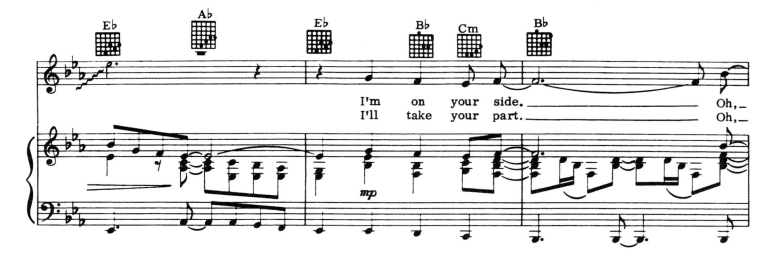

I'm on your side. _____ Oh, _
I'll take your part. _____ Oh, _

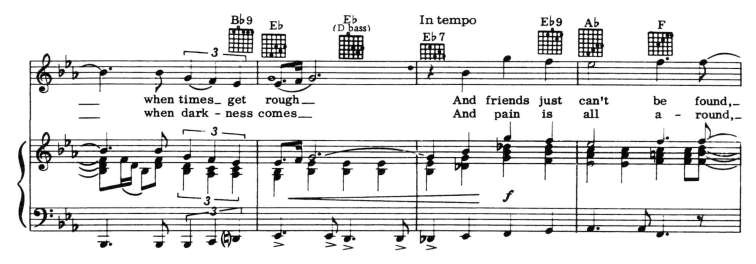

In tempo

_ when times_ get rough _ And friends just can't be found, _
when dark - ness comes _ And pain is all a - round, _

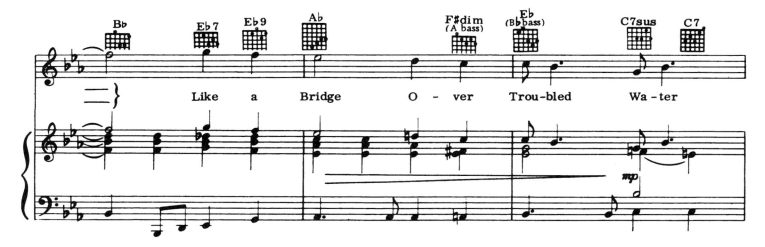

Like a Bridge O - ver Trou-bled Wa-ter

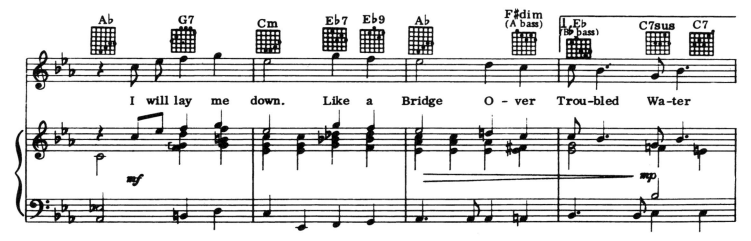

I will lay me down. Like a Bridge O - ver Trou-bled Wa-ter

3

I will lay me down.

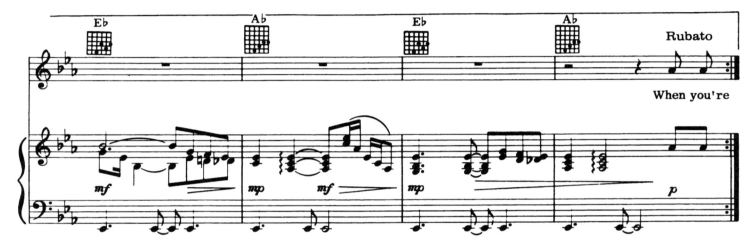

When you're

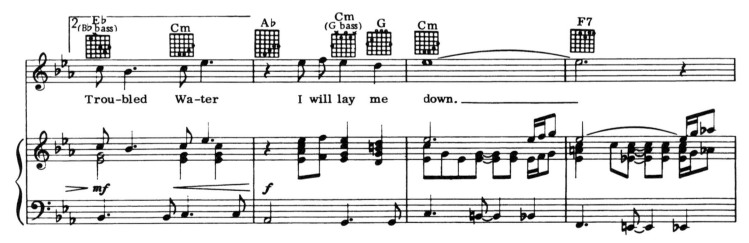

Trou-bled Wa-ter I will lay me down. _____

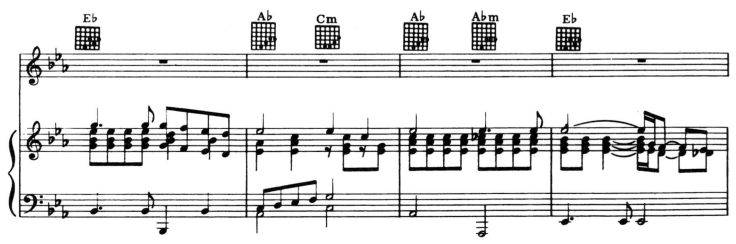

4

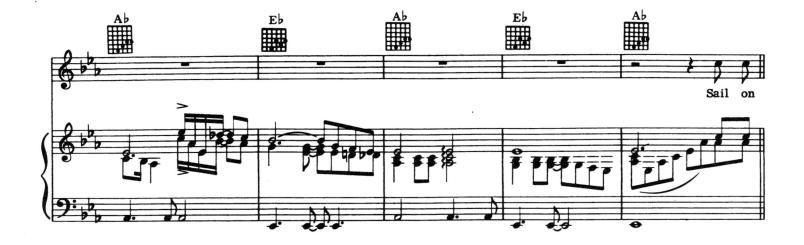

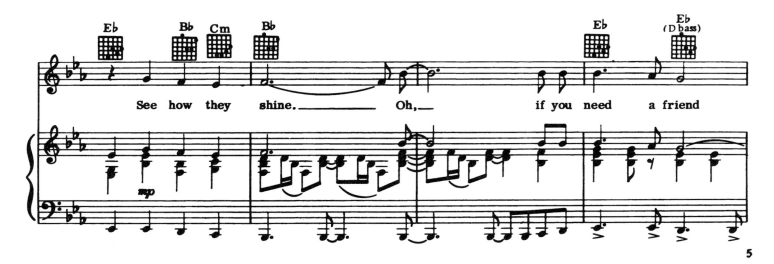

5

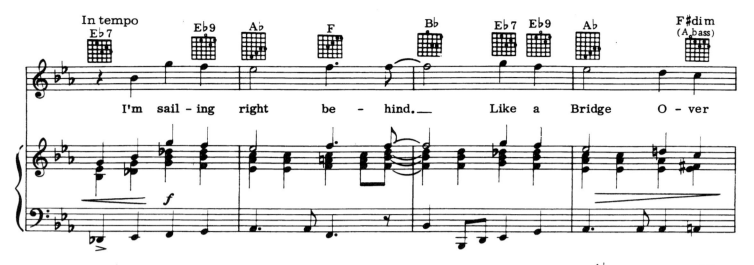

El Condor Pasa

Musical Arrangement by
J. MILCHBERG and D. ROBLES

English Lyric by
PAUL SIMON

swan that's here and gone. A man gets tied up to the ground, He gives the world its sad-dest

sound, its sad-dest sound.— I'd rath-er be a for-est than a

street. Yes I would. If I could,— I sure-ly would.— I'd rath-er feel the earth be-neath my

feet.. Yes I would. If I on-ly could,— I sure-ly would.—

Cecilia

Words and Music by
PAUL SIMON

Moderate, not too fast, rhythmically

Cel - ia, you're break-ing my heart, You're shak-ing my con - fi-dence dai-

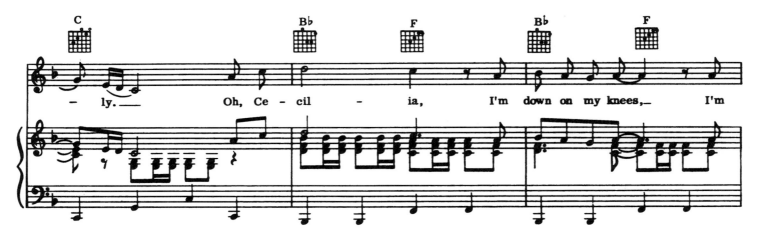

- ly. Oh, Ce - cil - ia, I'm down on my knees, I'm

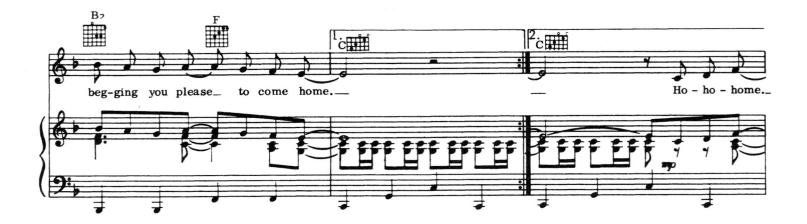

beg-ging you please___ to come home.___   Ho - ho - home.___

Mak - ing love___ in the af - ter - noon___ with Ce - ci -

- lia, Up in my___ bed - room,___ (mak - ing love_____) I got up___ to wash___

___ my face___ When I come back to bed,___ some-one's tak - en my place.___

Cel - ia, You're break-ing my heart,___ You're shak-ing my con - fi - dence dai -

- ly. Oh, Ce - cil - ia, I'm down on my knees,___ I'm

beg-ging you please___ to come home.___ Come on home.___ Poh poh

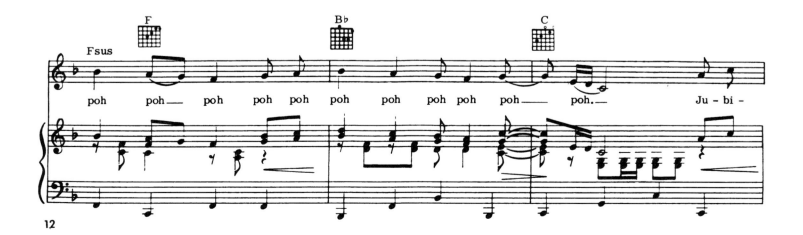

poh poh___ poh poh poh poh poh poh poh poh poh___ poh.___ Ju - bi -

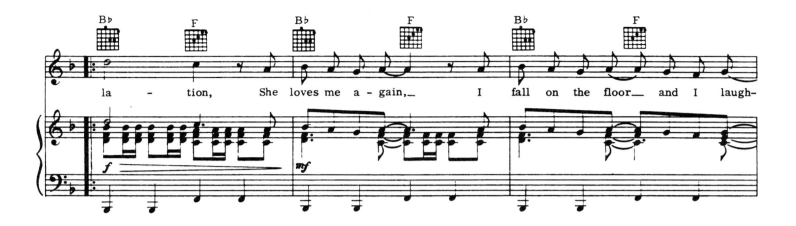

la - tion, She loves me a - gain,__ I fall on the floor__ and I laugh-

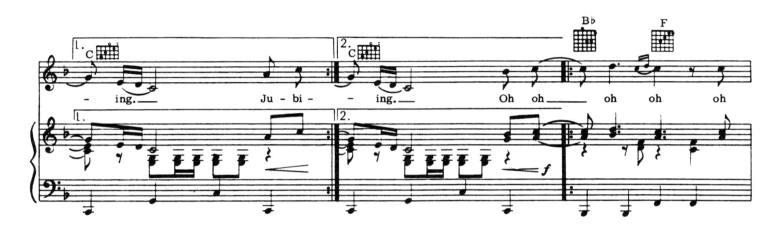

-ing.__ Ju - bi - -ing. Oh oh__ oh oh oh

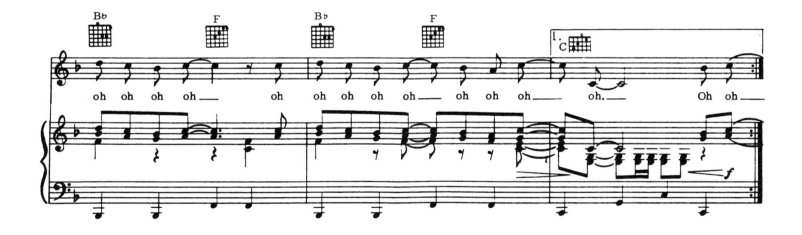

oh oh oh oh__ oh oh oh oh oh__ oh oh oh__ oh. Oh oh__

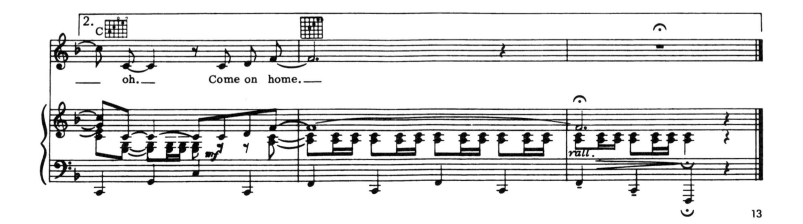

__ oh.__ Come on home.__

Keep The Customer Satisfied

Words and Music by
PAUL SIMON

Gee but it's great to be back home,   Home is where I want to
Dep - u - ty Sher - iff said to me   Tell me what you come here

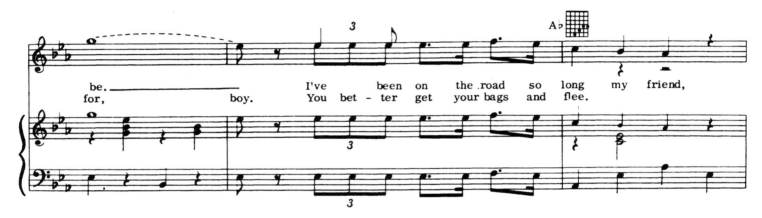

be. _____   I've been on the road so long my friend,
for, _____ boy.   You bet - ter get your bags and flee.

And if you came a - long I know you could - n't dis - a - gree. ___ It's the same old
You're in trou - ble boy, And now you're head - ing in - to more. ___ It's the same old

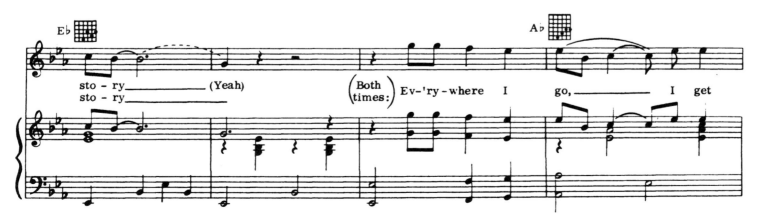

sto - ry _____ (Yeah)
sto - ry _____   (Both times:) Ev - 'ry - where I go, _____ I get

14

slan - dered, Li - beled,___ I hear words___ I nev - er heard In the Bi -

- ble.___ And I'm one step a - head of the shoe shine, Two steps a - way from the

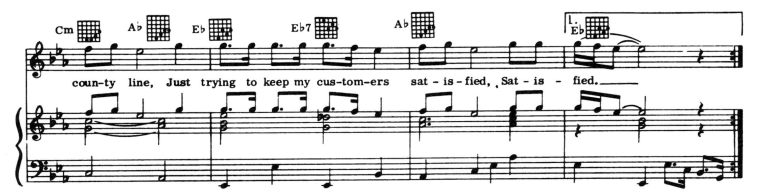

coun - ty line, Just trying to keep my cus - tom - ers sat - is - fied, Sat - is - fied.___

fied.___ Woh ___ Woh ___

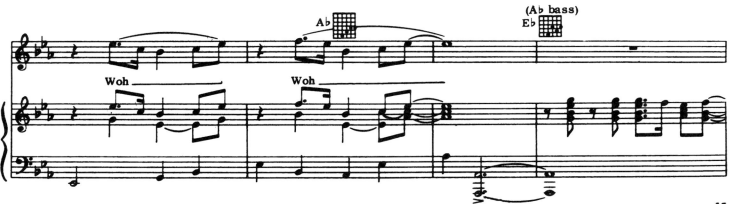

Woh ___ Woh ___

But it's the same old sto - ry _____

Ev - 'ry-where I go, _____ I get slan-dered, Li - beled, _ I hear words.

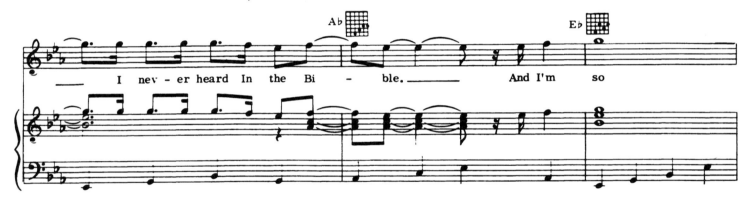

_____ I nev - er heard In the Bi - ble. _____ And I'm so

tired, _____ I'm oh _____ so tired, _____ But I'm

trying to keep my cus-tom-ers sat - is - fied, Sat - is - fied. _____

So Long, Frank Lloyd Wright

Words and Music by
PAUL SIMON

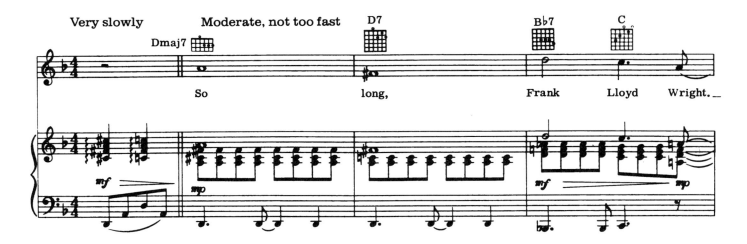

17

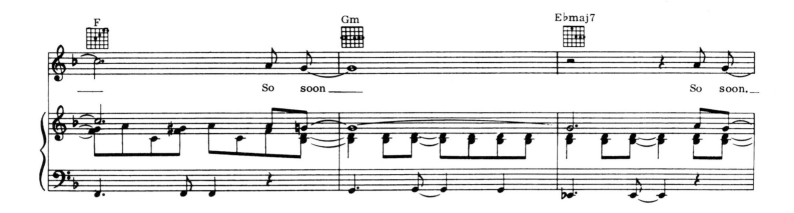

So soon ___   So soon. ___

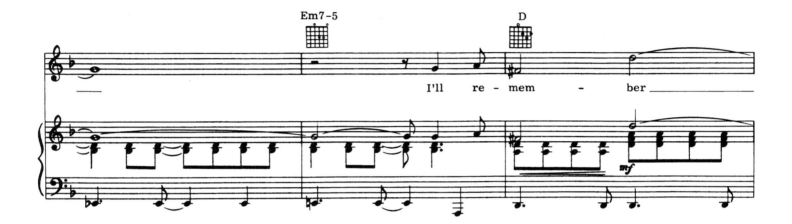

___   I'll re - mem - ber ___

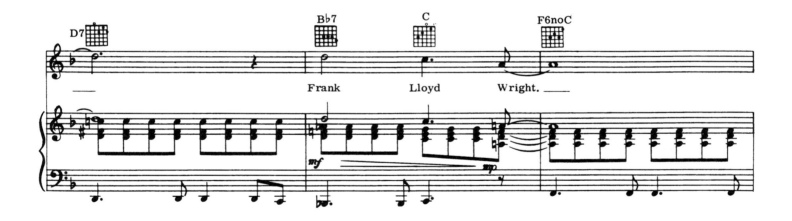

___ F   Frank   Lloyd   Wright. ___

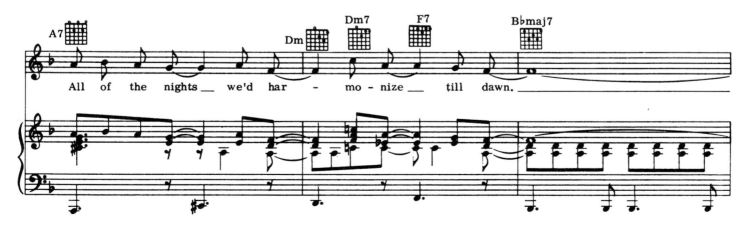

All of the nights ___ we'd har - mo - nize ___ till dawn. ___

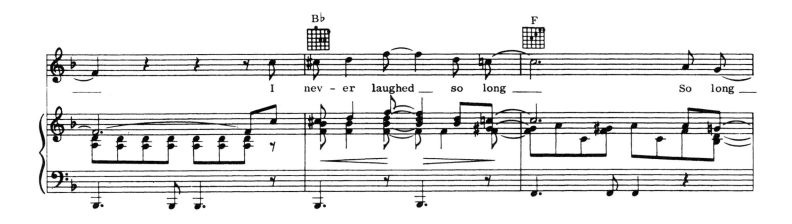

I nev-er laughed _ so long _ So long _

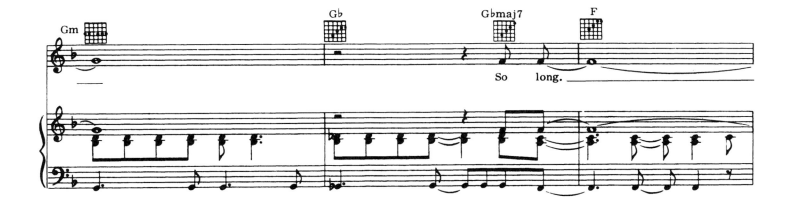

So long. _

Ar-chi-tects may come and Ar-chi-tects may go and nev-

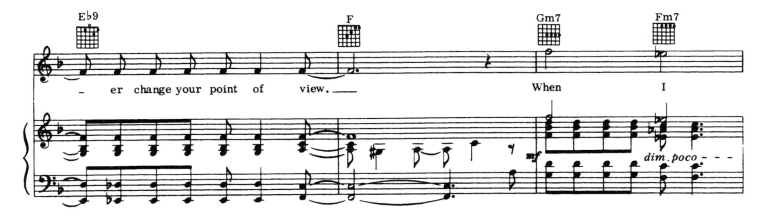

er change your point of view. _ When I

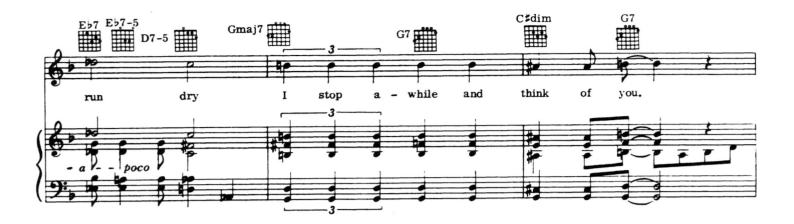

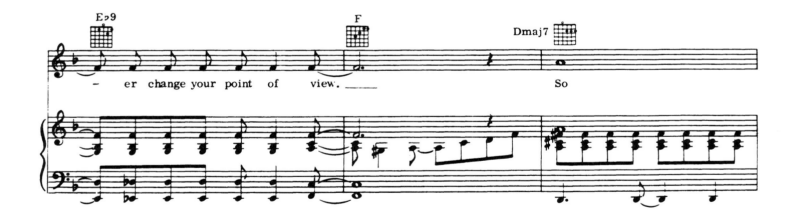

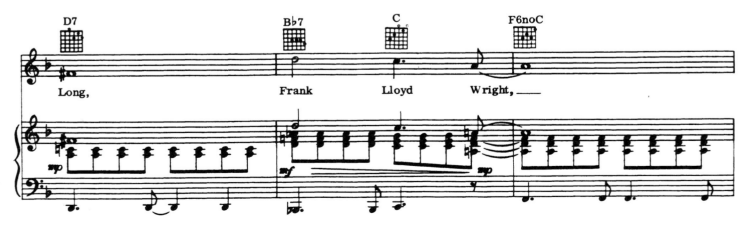

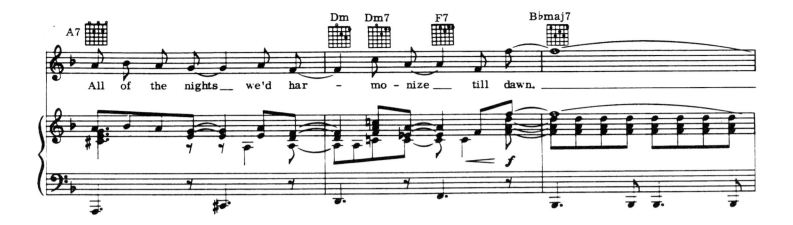

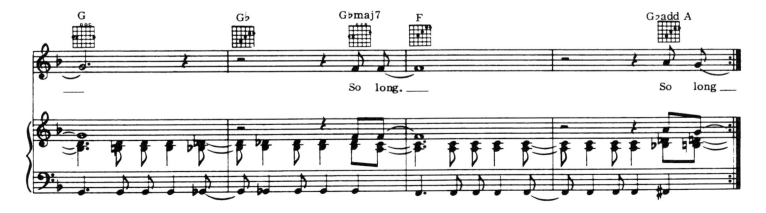

The Boxer

Words and Music by
PAUL SIMON

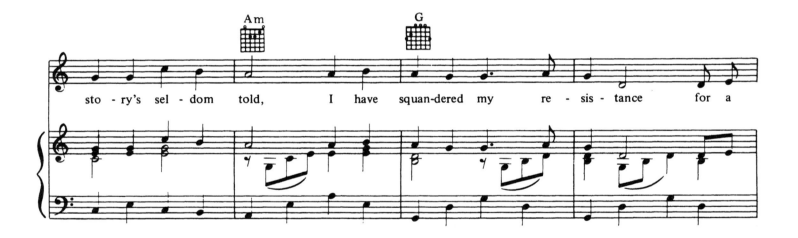

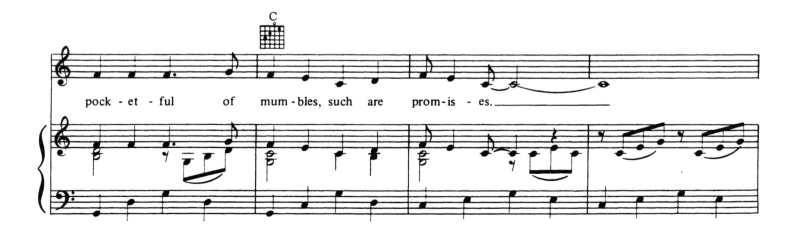

All lies and jest, still a man hears what he wants to hear,___ And

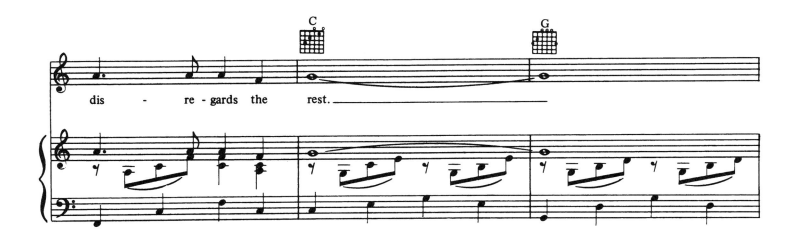

dis - re - gards the rest.___

When I left my home and my fam - i - ly,___ I was

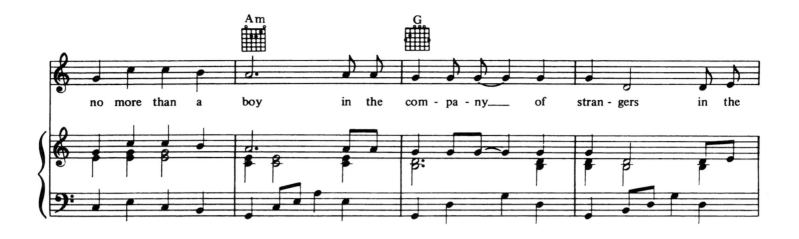

no more than a boy in the com - pa - ny___ of stran - gers in the

qui - et of a rail - way sta - tion run - ning scared, ___

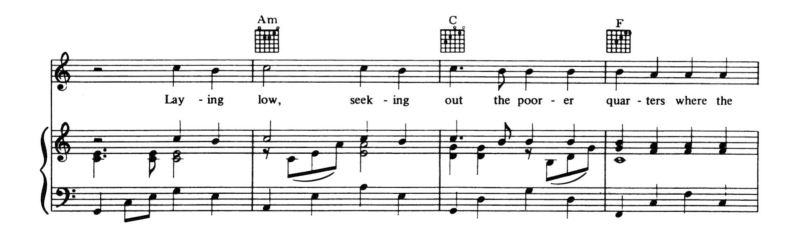

Lay - ing low, seek - ing out the poor - er quar - ters where the

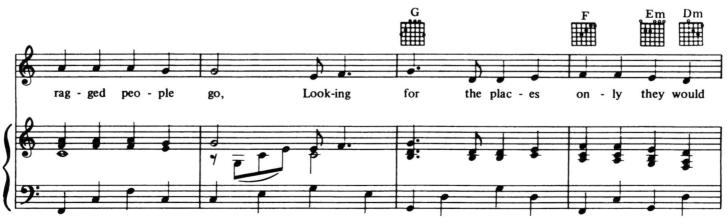

rag - ged peo - ple go, Look - ing for the plac - es on - ly they would

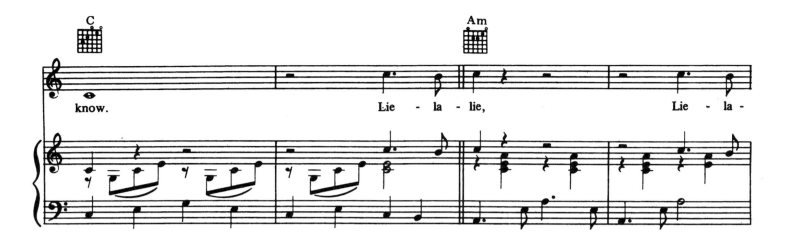

know. Lie - la - lie, Lie - la -

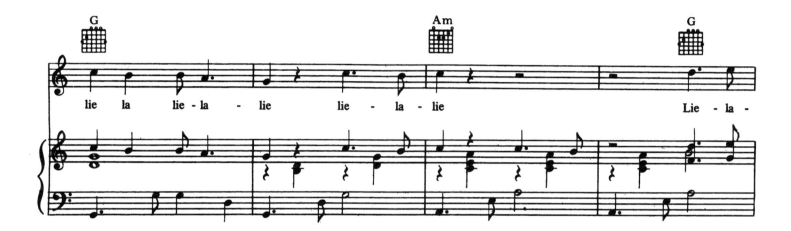

lie la lie - la - lie lie - la - lie Lie - la -

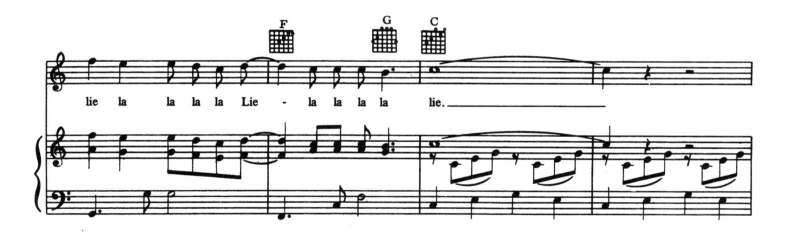

lie la la la la Lie - la la la la lie._____

Ask - ing on - ly work - man's wag - es I come

look-ing for a job, but I get no of - fers, _____ Just a

come-on from the whores___ on Sev-enth Av - e - nue._____

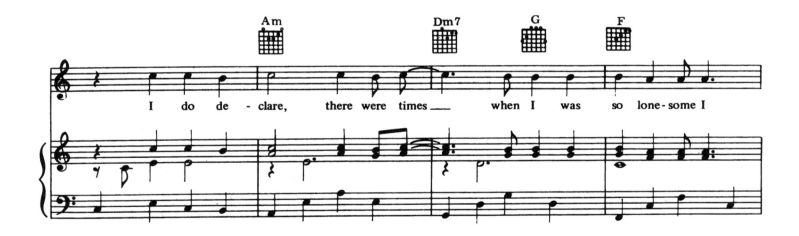

I do de -clare, there were times___ when I was so lone-some I

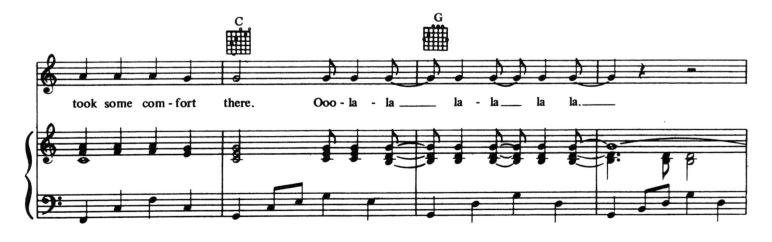

took some com-fort there. Ooo - la - la ___ la - la ___ la la.___

Then I'm lay - ing out my

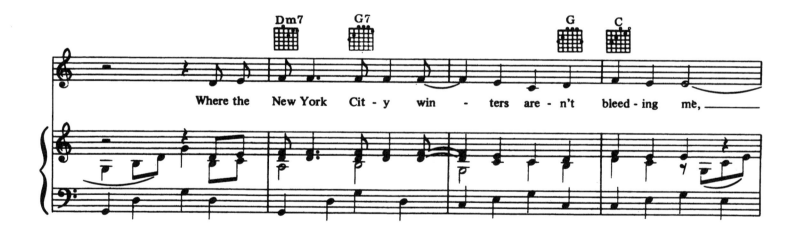

win - ter clothes___ and wish - ing I was gone,___ go - ing home

Where the New York Cit - y win - ters are - n't bleed - ing me,___

Lead - ing me,___

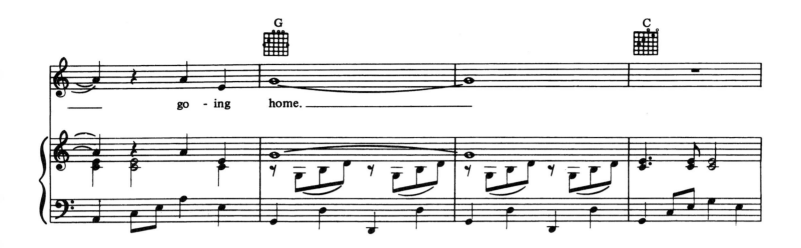

go - ing home.

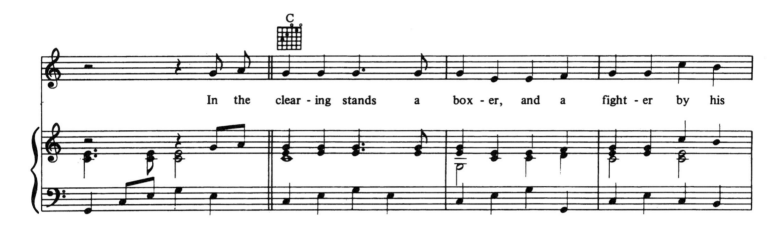

In the clear - ing stands a box - er, and a fight - er by his

trade, And he car - ries the re - mind - ers of ev - 'ry glove that

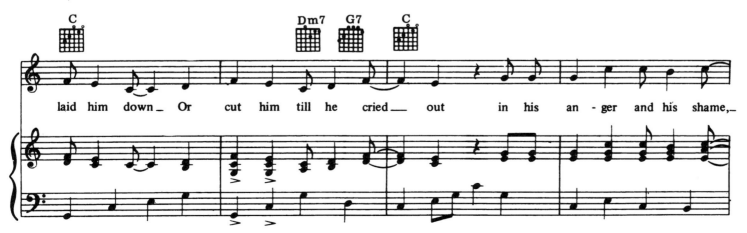

laid him down_ Or cut him till he cried_ out in his an - ger and his shame,_

28

"I am leav-ing, I am leav-ing." But the fight - er still re-mains.

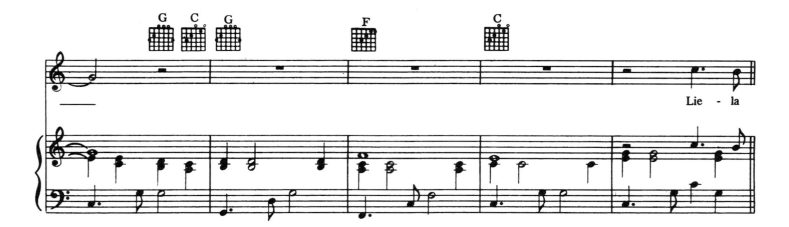

Lie - la

Fade

lie,   Lie - la - lie la lie -la - lie   Lie - la - lie

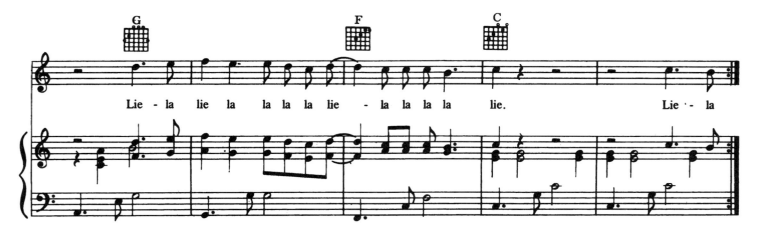

Lie - la lie la la la la lie - la la la la lie.   Lie - la

Baby Driver

Words and Music by
PAUL SIMON

Moderate bright tempo

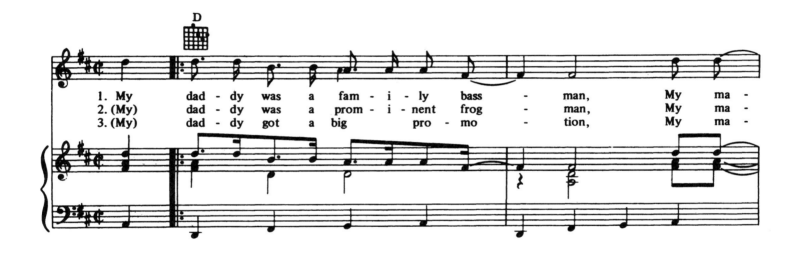

1. My dad-dy was a fam-i-ly bass-man, My ma-
2. (My) dad-dy was a prom-i-nent frog-man, My ma-
3. (My) dad-dy got a big pro-mo-tion, My ma-

ma was an en-gi-neer,___ And I___ was born___ one dark___
ma's in the Na-val re-serve;___ When I___ was young___ I car-
ma got a raise in pay,___ There's no___ one home,___ we're all___

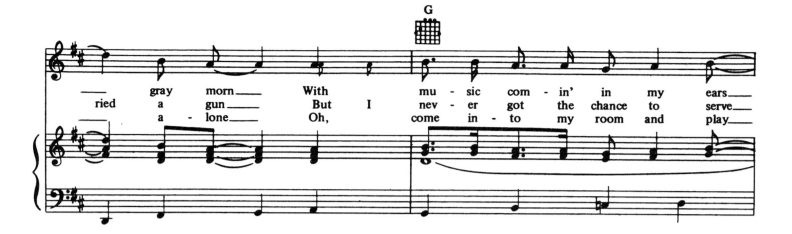

G

ried   gray   morn___   With | mu - sic   com - in'   in   my   ears___
ried   a   gun___   But   I | nev - er   got   the   chance   to   serve___
a - lone___   Oh, | come   in - to   my   room   and   play___

D

___   In   my   ears.___   They   call___
___   I   did   not   serve.___   They   call___
___   Yes,   we   can   play.___   I'm   not   talk -

G

___   me   Ba - by   Driv - er,   And   once___   u - pon   a   pair   of   wheels___
___   me   Ba - by   Driv - er,   And   once___   u - pon   a   pair   of   wheels___
___   in'   a - bout   your   pig - tails,   But   talk - in'   'bout   your   sex   ap - peal___

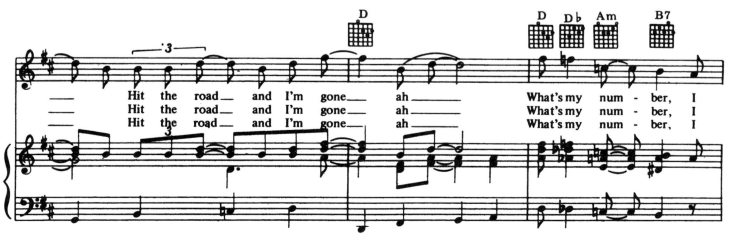

D   **D** **Db** **Am** **B7**

___   Hit   the   road___   and   I'm   gone___   ah___   What's   my   num - ber,   I
___   Hit   the   road___   and   I'm   gone___   ah___   What's   my   num - ber,   I
___   Hit   the   road___   and   I'm   gone___   ah___   What's   my   num - ber,   I

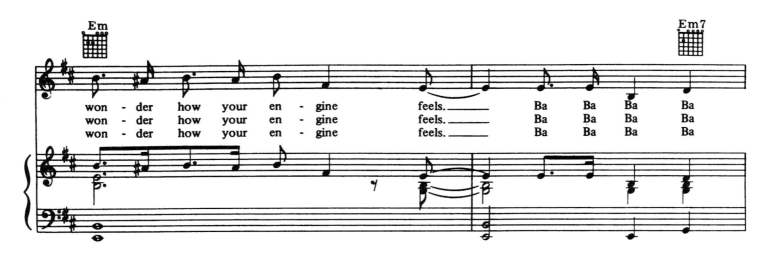

won - der how your en - gine feels. _____ Ba Ba Ba Ba
won - der how your en - gine feels. _____ Ba Ba Ba Ba
won - der how your en - gine feels. _____ Ba Ba Ba Ba

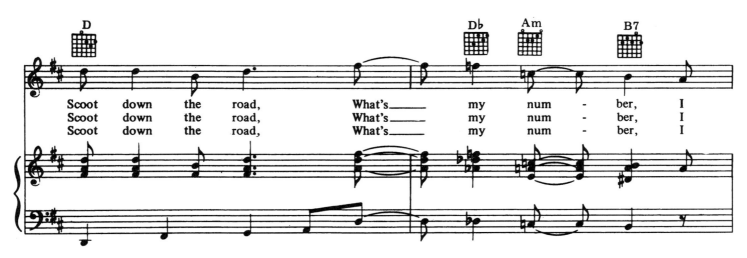

Scoot down the road, What's_____ my num - ber, I
Scoot down the road, What's_____ my num - ber, I
Scoot down the road, What's_____ my num - ber, I

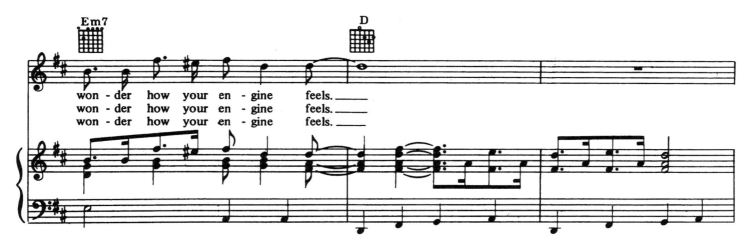

won - der how your en - gine feels. _____
won - der how your en - gine feels. _____
won - der how your en - gine feels. _____

1, 2.   3.

2. My
3. My

Repeat and fade

The Only Living Boy In New York

Words and Music by
PAUL SIMON

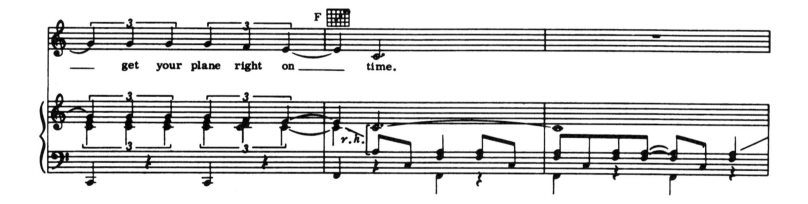

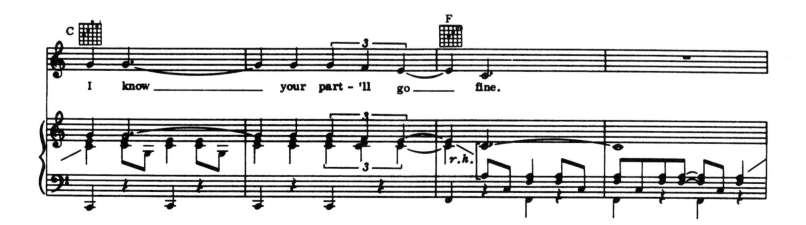

Fly _____ down to Mex - i - co. _____

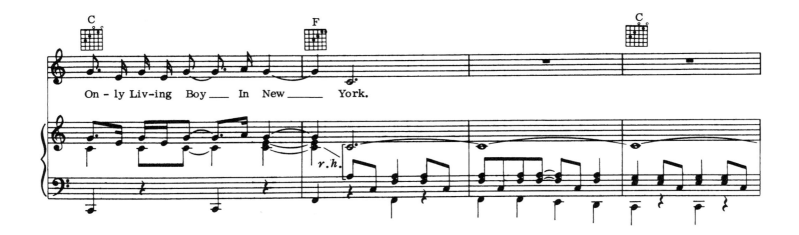

Da - n-da - da - n-da - da - n-da - da ___ and here I am, _____ The

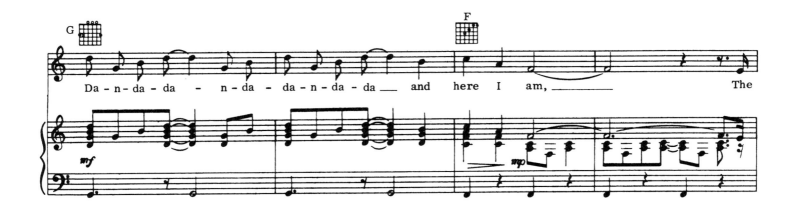

On - ly Liv-ing Boy ___ In New _____ York.

I ___ get the news I need ___ from the weath-er re - port. ___

I _____ can gath-er all the news I need ____ from the weath-er re - port. ____

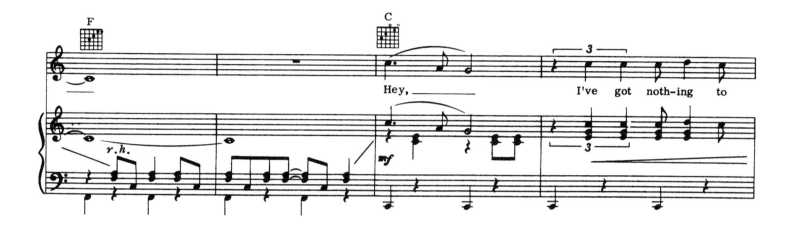

_____ Hey, _____ I've got noth-ing to

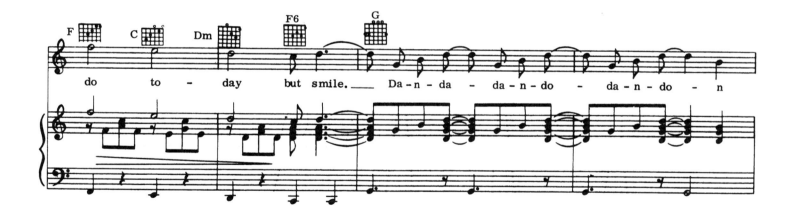

do to - day but smile. ____ Da - n - da - da - n - do - da - n - do - n

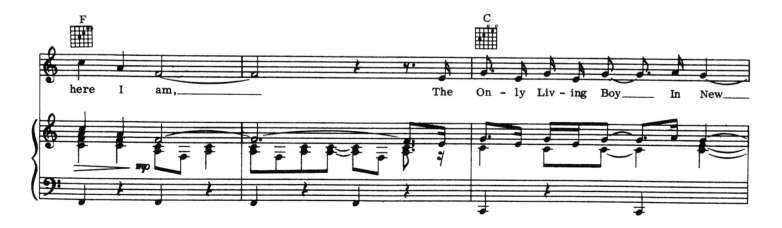

here I am, _____ The On - ly Liv - ing Boy ____ In New ____

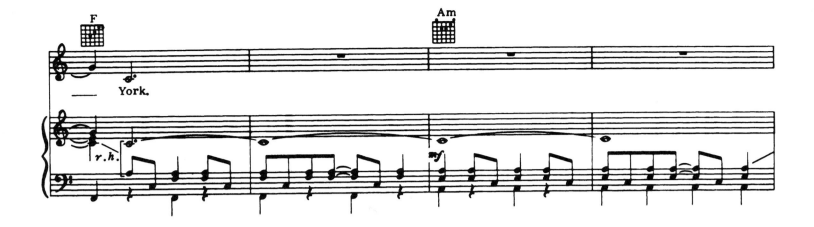

York.

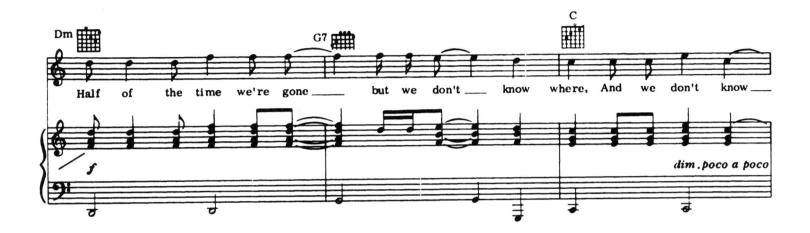

Half of the time we're gone ____ but we don't ____ know where, And we don't know ____

dim. poco a poco

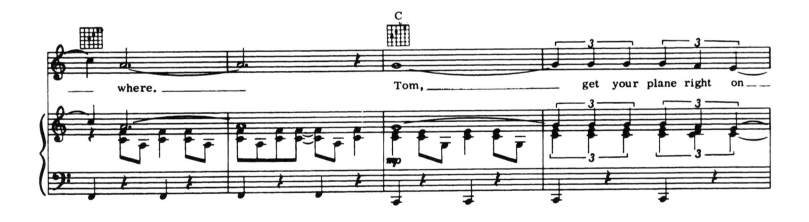

____ where. ____ Tom, ____ get your plane right on ____

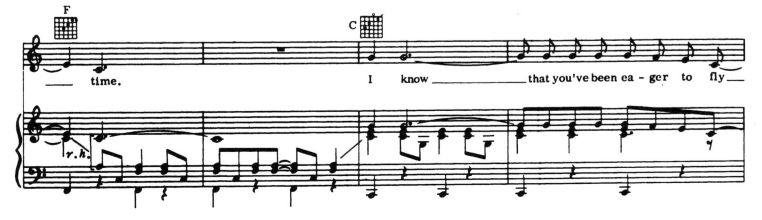

____ time. I know ____ that you've been ea - ger to fly ____

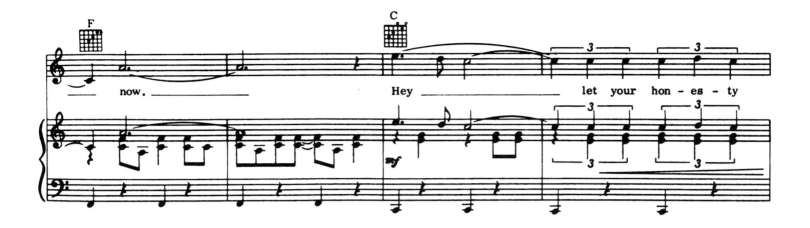

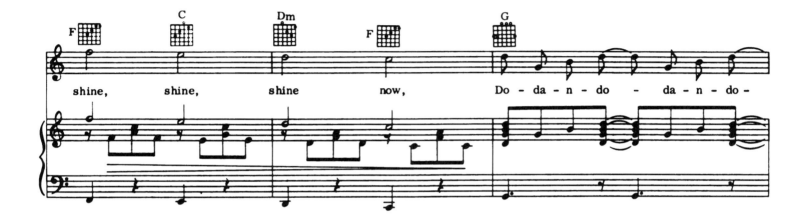

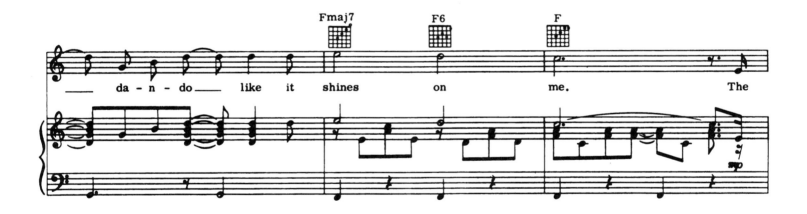

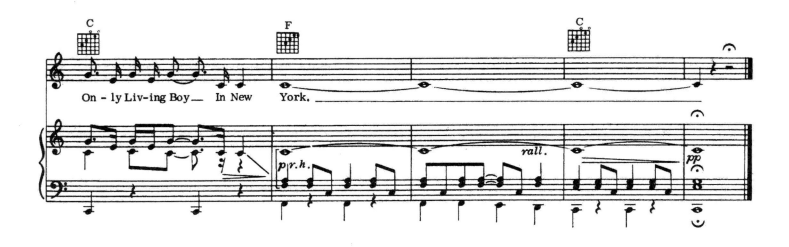

Why Don't You Write Me?

Words and Music by
PAUL SIMON

Moderate, with a strong beat

Why Don't You Write ___ Me? I'm out ___ in the jun - gle, I'm hun-

- gry to hear ___ you.   Send me a card, ___ I am wait-

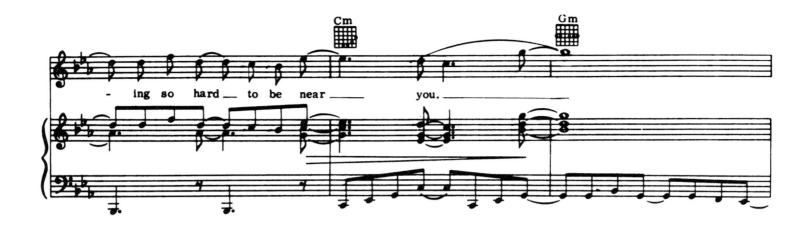

-ing so hard to be near you.

(Falsetto:) La la la. (Basso) Why don't you write? Some-thing is wrong

and I know I got to be there. (yeah)

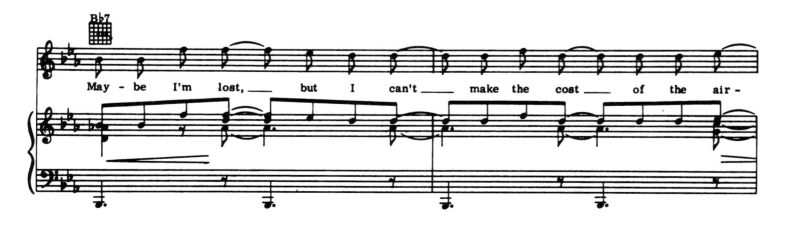

May-be I'm lost, but I can't make the cost of the air-

fare.___ (oo)___ Tell me why___ Why___

Tell me why___ Why___ Why___
Why___

Why Don't You Write___ Me? A let - ter would bright - en my lone -

- li - est eve - ning. Mail it to - day___ if it's on -

- ly to say___ that you're leav - ing me.___ (Oo)___

(Falsetto:) La la ___ la.

(Sing:) Mon-day morn - ing, sit - ting in the sun Hop ___ ing and wish-ing for the mail ___ to come.

Tues-day, nev - er got a word, mmm.___ Wednes-day, Thurs-day, ain't no sign, Drank___

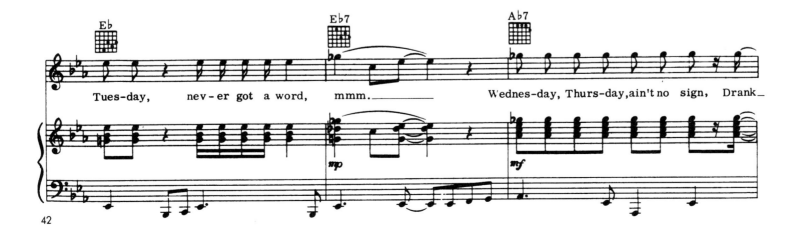

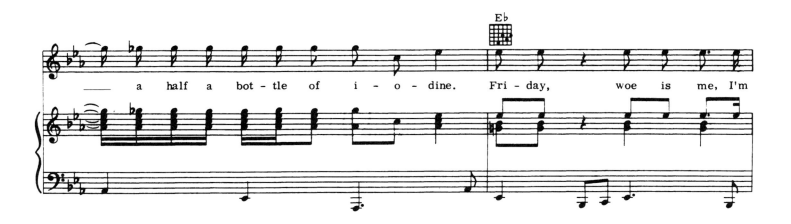

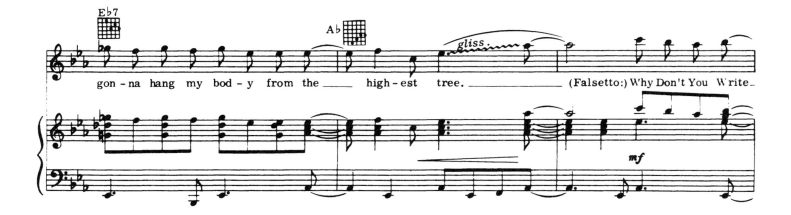

Bye Bye, Love

By FELICE BRYANT and
BOUDLEAUX BRYANT

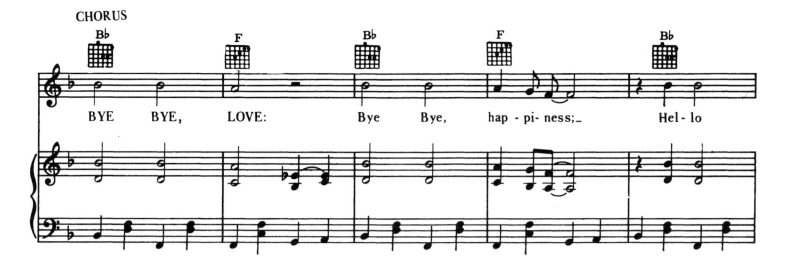

CHORUS

BYE BYE, LOVE: Bye Bye, hap-pi-ness;_ Hel-lo

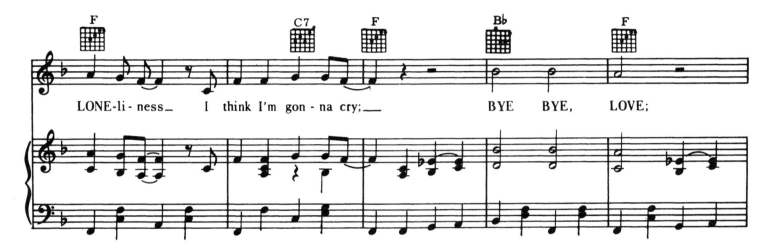

LONE-li-ness_ I think I'm gon-na cry;_ BYE BYE, LOVE;

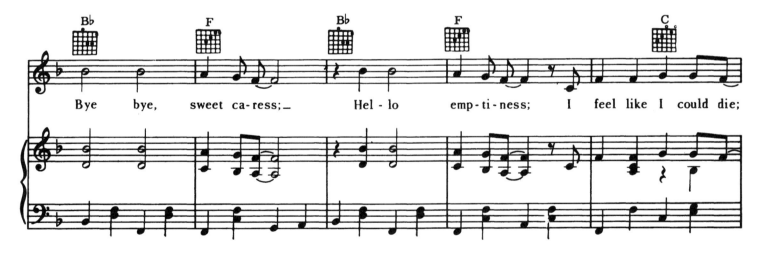

Bye bye, sweet ca-ress;_ Hel-lo emp-ti-ness; I feel like I could die;

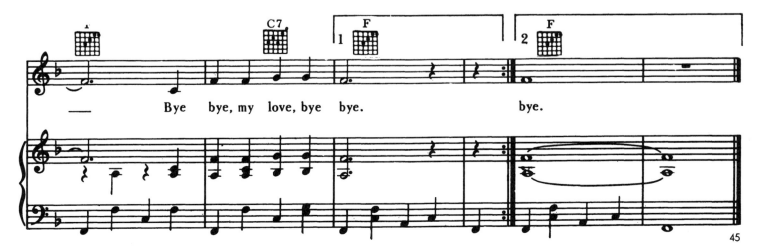

Bye bye, my love, bye bye. bye.

Song For The Asking

Words and Music by
PAUL SIMON

wait - ing ___ all my ___ life. ___

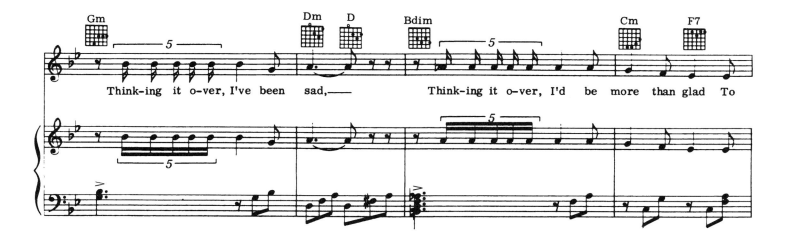

Think-ing it o-ver, I've been sad, ___ Think-ing it o-ver, I'd be more than glad To

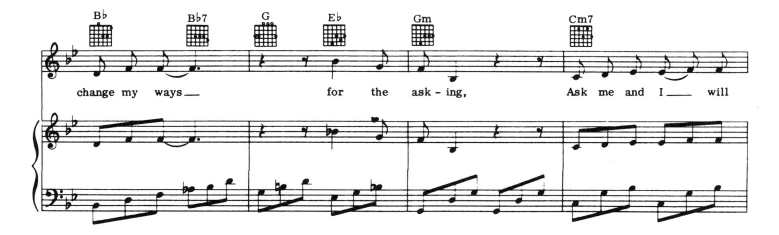

change my ways ___ for the ask - ing, Ask me and I ___ will

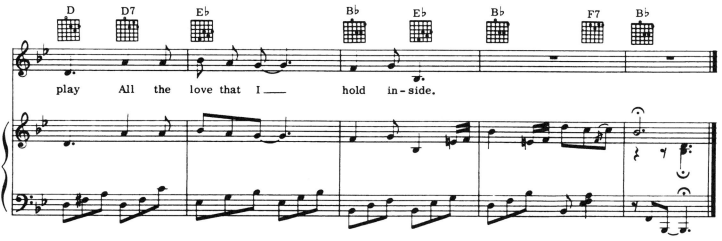

play All the love that I ___ hold in - side.